The Guide To Visiting Cancun

Isaac G. Cox

Introduction

This book is a comprehensive handbook that unlocks the captivating wonders of Cancun, Mexico. This guidebook serves as a virtual compass, directing travelers to immerse themselves in Cancun's myriad of attractions, activities, and practical travel information.

Starting with the "See" section, the guide introduces readers to the must-visit destinations in Cancun. From the ancient ruins of Tulum and the awe-inspiring Chichen Itza to the scenic Xcaret Park and the charming Malecon Tajamar, readers are guided to explore the city's historical, cultural, and natural gems. The guide also presents unique experiences such as the Turtle Hatchery and the stunning Playa Delfines, ensuring travelers don't miss out on Cancun's beauty.

The "Hear" section takes readers on a musical journey through Cancun's nightlife. From the vibrant Mariachi Dinner Shows and the iconic Coco Bongo to the rhythm of the Grand Mambo Cafe and the Tu Cafe, readers are encouraged to tap into Cancun's lively and diverse music scene. The guide also introduces Plaza de Toros, offering a unique bullring experience.

For those who love to savor culinary delights, the "Eat" section is a gastronomic treasure map. La Terraza del Vino, Du Mexique, Picus, and Terra Nostra are highlighted, offering travelers a taste of Cancun's diverse cuisine. Additionally, the guide introduces Chikle Prehispanic Cooking Classes and Taco Tours, enabling readers to immerse themselves in local flavors.

Cancun's vibrant nightlife takes center stage in the "Drink" section. The Tequila Herradura Sensorial Museum, Las de Guanatos, The Surfin' Burrito, and El Rincon del Vino are showcased, inviting readers to experience Cancun's unique beverages. The guide also introduces the traditional drink Horchata and the Isla Brewing Company for those seeking a memorable drinking experience.

Readers seeking memorable experiences will find their desires met in the "Experience" section. From high-flying adventures like Jetpack Adventures and diving at the Cancun Underwater Museum to more relaxed activities such as swimming in a cenote or cuddling a crocodile, Cancun offers a diverse range of experiences for all types of travelers. The guide also presents Selvatica's ATV and Zipline Adventures, horseback riding at Rancho Baaxal, and the exhilarating opportunity to swim with whale sharks.

For those yearning for relaxation, the "Relax & Chill" section provides a tranquil escape. Parque Kabah, Leblanc Spa Resort, Xbalamque, and beach yoga classes offer travelers a chance to unwind. The guide also introduces Garrafon Natural Reef Park and Isla Mujeres as serene destinations to rejuvenate.

The "Hostels & Hospitality Exchanges" section offers insights into budget-friendly accommodations, ensuring every traveler can find suitable lodging. The "Traveling Knowledge" section provides practical information on essentials like checklists, language, currency, visas, and communication. Travelers can also refer to information about operating hours, tipping, and getting around Cancun.

In essence, this is an all-encompassing companion that empowers travelers to explore, engage, and savor every facet of Cancun's beauty, culture, and adventure. With detailed insights, vibrant recommendations, and practical guidance, this guidebook invites readers to embark on an unforgettable journey to Cancun.

Contents

See

Cancun is known for its glitzy resorts, turquoise waters, white sand beaches and high end seafood restaurants - but there's more to this Mexican holiday destination than meets the eye.

Beyond the fruity cocktails and sun loungers, Cancun offers something for everyone. If you have had your fill of lounging around the pool, you can stuff your face on fresh authentic tacos at a local street food cart, dance the night away at a salsa club, go birdwatching in a national park, enjoy thrilling watersports or even swim with whale sharks.

Look deeper beneath the surface and you will find ancient Mayan ruins that tell the story of a fascinating civilization. Or, head off the beaten track and visit small villages to get a real taste of Mexican life. To really savor all of the flavor of Cancun - here are some of the top things to see.

Tulum

Tulum Municipality, Carretera federal Chetumal - Cancún km. 230, Tulum, QROO, Mexico
20.2148° N, 87.4293° W

The entire Yucatan Peninsula is rich with ancient Mayan history and Tulum is one of the most impressive sights. Only a two hour drive from Cancun, it's an easy day trip and several travel agencies offer guided visits. You can view the ruins, then sink your toes into the fine sand or cool off in the water.

All along the sugary-sand coastline, swept with warm breezes, are dramatic Mayan ruins on cliffs overlooking the pale azure waters of the Caribbean Sea. Capture photos of this striking historical site, which used to be a crucial trading post.

Chichen Itza

8am to 4:30pm
Yucatan Region
20.6843° N, 88.5678° W

UNESCO preserved the Pre-Hispanic city of Chichen Itza for its "Outstanding Universal Value" and when you walk through this sprawling complex of ruins it is easy to see why. The town was built here because of the cenotes: deep wells tapping into underground waters below the arid Yucatan Peninsula.

The city was one of the most diverse in the Mayan World, which is likely why the architecture here is so varied. Although it has deteriorated since it was abandoned in the 15th century, these imposing structures still invoke awe. One of the most visited archeological sites in all of Mexico, you may choose to visit on a day trip from Cancun or stay overnight to explore it more deeply.

Xcaret Park Scenic Tower - Torre Escenica

+52 800 292 2738 - 8:30am to 9pm - xcaret.com.mx
Carretera Chetúmal-Puerto Juárez Kilómetro 282, Solidaridad, 77710 Playa del Carmen
20° 34' 51.2868" N 87° 7' 10.9128" W

Photo By Serge Melki from Indianapolis, USA (Cancun Vista Tower) [CC BY 2.0] via Wikimedia Commons

Get your bearings and see a bird's eye view of Cancun from the top of this scenic tower. You'll feel a rush in your stomach as the elevator lifts you up 260 feet above the city. The expansive viewing platform rotates 360 degrees and offers stunning views of the sunlight glinting on the waters of the Riviera Maya.

You can even see as far as Cozumel Island on the horizon and spot many Cancun landmarks such as the St. Francis of Assisi Chapel, the Gran Tlachco Theater and the lagoon.

Malecon Tajamar

+52 984 168 8889
Av Malecón Fonatur, Zona Hotelera, 77500 Cancún, Q.R., Mexico
21° 8' 44.5164" N86° 48' 53.0784" W

Image Source: tajamarcancun.com

This gorgeous waterfront promenade is one of the most scenic areas in Cancun. Take a stroll along the sparkling Nichupte lagoon and admire the sweeping views of the Hotel Zone skyline. It is a popular spot for jogging and practicing yoga and there are also several superb restaurants and cafes where you can grab a bite with a view.

If you are up early enough, this is one of the best places to see the sunrise as you start your day. Or, enjoy the seaside at sunset and sip cocktails while you savor the refreshing evening breeze.

Turtle Hatchery (Turtugranja)

+52 998 888 0705 - 9am to 5pm - facebook.com/Tortugranja.mx
Carretera Sac Bajo Km 5 Isla Mujeres, Mexico
21° 13' 16.9788" N 86° 43' 54.3468" W

Have you ever seen an albino turtle before? You can see one of these strange ancient white reptiles at the Turtle Hatchery on Isla Mujeres. It is small,uncrowded and offers you the opportunity to get up close with a range of turtles in all sizes, shapes and ages.

This quirky little reptile zoo is a great budget attraction - it only costs 30 pesos to get in. It was created by a local fisherman in the 1980s, who wanted to protect endangered sea turtles from being killed for their meat and eggs. If you are lucky you might be visiting on a day when the baby turtles are released into the sea. You can also check out other creatures here, such as the small community of iguanas who sun themselves on the pile of rocks near the front entrance.

Playa Delfines

+52 481 380 7951
Boulevard Kukulkan Kilometer 19.5, Zona Hotelera, 77500 Cancún, Q.R., Mexico
21° 2' 49.1316" N 86° 46' 57.6372" W

The turquoise water laps against a long stretch of soft white sand as far as the eye can see on this stunning beach. It's one of the most loved areas of the coastline in Cancun and it's conveniently accessible from the Hotel Zone.

Bring your camera to snap inspiring shots of the sugary sand, pale blue water and dramatic skies. Grabbing a photo of the iconic "Cancun" sign along the waterfront is a must to add to social media and make your friends jealous. It's also a great place to bring the kids, with multiple play areas to run and scramble on. Don't forget the sunscreen!

The Maya Museum

+52 998 885 3843 - 9am to 6pm - inah.gob.mx
Blvd. Kukulcan km 16.5, Zona Hotelera
21° 8' 6.2844" N 86° 45' 15.066" W

Image Source - David Stanley

The Mayan civilisation is pretty amazing - they were noted for having the only known written language in MesoAmerica, were astute astronomers and were the first to develop cocoa for consumption (thanks Pakal!). Maya culture still exists and there are more than 7 million Mayans still living in the region.

You can get a refresher on Mayan history by visiting the Maya Museum, located near the archaeological site of San Miguelito. It has a fascinating collection, including an exhibition room on the Mayan population that lived in Quintana Roo. You will be able to see room after room filled with Mayan architecture and artifacts. One of the most impressive sights at the museum is human skeletal remains that were discovered in an underwater cave in Tulum and are thought to be approximately 14,000 years old.

Xcaret Park

+52 800 292 2738 - 8:30am to 9pm - xcaret.com.mx
Carretera Chetúmal-Puerto Juárez Kilómetro 282, Solidaridad, 77710 Playa del Carmen
20° 34' 51.2868" N 87° 7' 10.9128" W

By AMAPO - Own work, CC BY-SA 3.0

One of the most strange and fascinating experiences you will have in Cancun; Xcaret Park should certainly be on your list. This archeological park in Riviera Maya offers you the chance to visit a coral reef aquarium, watch a musical show telling the story of Mexico's history before European explorers and reenactments of a pre-Hispanic ball game played by Mayan people.

You can also see the dazzling plumage of the Scarlet Macaws - Xcaret broke the Guinness Record for having 132 of these rainbow-feathered birds born in the same place!

Hear

Music is a huge part of Mexican culture. Every night when the sun goes down, the streets of Cancun come alive with soulful guitar strains, pumping dance beats, lively horn solos - a thrilling orchestra of sound from every direction!

From traditional Mariachi music to sensual salsa to pumping dance beats, there are many opportunities to listen to the melody of Mexico. Here are some of best spots in Cancun to get your groove on.

Mariachi Dinner Shows

+52 998 848 8220 - 2pm to 10:30pm - haciendasisal.com
Hacienda Sisal Restaurant, Blvd. Kukulcán, km 13.5, Zona Hotelera, 77500 Cancún, QROO, México
21° 5' 29.1588" N 86° 46' 16.8312" W

By Gerardo Gonzalez [CC BY 2.0], via Wikimedia Commons

Mariachi performers are so intrinsically important to Mexico's culture that they were designated UNESCO World Heritage in the intangible culture category. These musicians light up every fiesta, wedding, funeral and birthday with rousing tunes played at full volume on trumpets, guitars, violins, vihuelas and guitarróns (large bodied six-string fretless bass guitar).

They are also known as the messengers of love and young men often hire them to serenade their romantic interests. It's impossible not to tap your toes to their jubilant, richly-layered and emotionally moving music.

Head to Hacienda Sisal Restaurant next to the Royal Sands Cancun to see a live Mariachi band perform as part of the Dinner Shows that are staged twice per week. Another place where you can see Mariachis is the Xcaret Park (mentioned above, number 8 under SEE), where they perform in the evening show, known as Xcaret de Noche.

Coco Bongo

+52 800 841 4636 - 10:30am to 5am - cocobongo.com
Blvd. Kukulcan Km. 9.5, Zona Hotelera, 77500 Cancún, Q.R., Mexico
21° 7' 57.7056" N 86° 44' 49.4448" W

Coco Bongo Spiderman. Photo by Abeeeer, CC License

Ready for a night of vibrant, spectacular performances? Coco Bongo is a legendary Cancun club that features an array of performances - including salsa bands and live rock.

You might even be lucky enough to see Kiss, Michael Jackson and Rihanna impersonators, flying acrobats or movie screenings. No matter what, it will always be fun and lively! A conga line will likely form at some point which might even head out the door for a quick spin around the street.

Grand Mambo Cafe

+52 998 884 4536 - 10:30pm to 3am - mambocafe.com.mx
Av Xcaret MZA 2 LTE 6 LOCAL 31, Benito Juárez, SM 35, 77505
Cancún, Q.R., Mexico
21° 9' 23.5044" N 86° 49' 51.2616" W

Cancun's biggest Latin music club, this exciting venue is popular with locals, expats and tourists. It features an exciting selection of live music, including bachata, cumbia and salsa.

If you arrive before midnight you will hear a DJ spinning recorded Latin music, after which the live shows will start after the clock strikes 12. It is open until 4am, so you can dance the night away, watch the sunrise and then collapse into bed tired and happy.

Tu Cafe

+52 998 110 0099 - 4pm to 11pm
Av. Yaxchilán near Av. Uxmal
21° 9' 1.0008" N 86° 49' 14.934" W

Image Source - Tripadvisor

Believe it or not, there is actually a local jazz and funk music scene in Cancun and it centers around this quirky and cool boho coffeehouse. It features open jazz/funk sessions on Tuesdays and screens intriguing independent films on Fridays.

It also hosts an array of rotating art exhibits, so it's a pretty interesting place for culture vultures to hang out. You can have a coffee and relax while soaking up the local art and music scene.

Plaza de Toros - Bullring

Av. Bonampak y Av. Sayil, Zona Hotelera, 77500 Cancún, QROO, Mexico
21° 9' 0.8568" N 86° 49' 15.3624" W

By Steven Depolo - Estocada Toreador Bullfight Plaza de Toros and Folkloric Show Cancun Mexico, CC BY 2.0

If you have never heard the roar of the crowd in a packed bullring, visiting Plaza de Toros will be unforgettable. Every Wednesday, this large bullfight arena comes to life with folkloric dances, live music and of course - a bullfight!

It's like nothing you have ever seen before and this captivating spectacle will have you cheering, gasping and watching through your fingers.

Eat

Look beyond the Starbucks and McDonald's - although some of Cancun has become filled with fast food names, there's still a food culture that is very much alive. There are some restaurants in which high quality food is taken very seriously, and Cancun has its fair share of superb fine dining joints, as well as down to earth authentic Mexican fare made with fresh ingredients.

Your best bet is to stay away from the tourist spots (when is this not sound advice) with their cheap drinks and lacklustre food. Instead, head to the non-chain dining spots or the joints that the locals love. Since you've traveled this far, be adventurous: bring your appetite and try something you've never had before!

La Terraza del Vino

+52 998 126 0131 - 6pm to 3am - facebook.com/laterrazadevino
Alcatraces 29 Super Manzana 22 Manzana 10 Lote 38 Cancun
Quintana Roo, 77500 Cancún, Q.R., Mexico
21° 9' 36.9108" N 86° 49' 39.6624" W

Image Source: Esteban D via Foursquare

This atmospheric wine bar is the perfect place for wowing that special someone, whether you have been together for years or you just met them earlier that night. During the day it hides behind unassuming garage doors, but when night falls it opens up into a lively terrace where you can sip wine and dine on mouthwatering tapas and gourmet pizza.

Live music played right outside the building sets the mood for a romantic evening, making this one of the best places for a date night in Cancun.

Du Mexique

+52 998 884 5889 - 7pm to 11pm - dumexique.com
Av. Bonampak 109, esq. calle Pargo, Sm.3, Centro, 77500, Cancún, Quintana Roo
21° 9' 39.2688" N 86° 49' 15.8232" W

When you step through the door of this luxurious restaurant, you will feel like you have been instantly transported from Mexico to France. At this superb and elegant spot, they whip up sophisticated classic French dishes with fresh ingredients from Mexico.

The chef, Alain Grimond, is from Lyon France and is known for greeting his patrons with a genuine, friendly hug and kiss on the cheek. Reservations are necessary, as this is one of Cancun's hottest eateries.

Picus

+52 998 129 6011 - 24 Hours - Facebook Page
Av. Rueda Medina (1 block northwest of ferry docks), Isla Mujeres, Mexico
21° 14' 25.7748" N 86° 44' 17.5524" W

Source: https://www.pinterest.com/ericapoirier/isla

Dining at this restaurant requires a short ferry ride over from Cancun. However, the oceanfront dining is completely worth the journey when you sink your toes into the sand and your teeth into fresh, juicy, tart ceviche.

Picus is known for casual and tasty lunches made with high quality ingredients, perfect for the low key vibe of Isla Mujeres. Try the hot tortilla chips they make themselves and wash it down with a mojito filled with plenty of lime and fresh mint.

Terra Nostra

+52 998 891 5700 - nizuc.com
NIZUC Resort and Spa, Blvd. Kukulkan, Punta Nizuc, 77500 Cancún, Quintana Roo
21° 2' 2.7492" N 86° 47' 20.67" W

This photo of NIZUC Resort and Spa is courtesy of TripAdvisor

If you want to treat yourself to a superb meal and you would like a break from Mexican cuisine, indulge in an atmospheric dining experience at Terra Nostra. This Mediterranean restaurant offers wood-oven baked specialties, homemade pasta and other delights made from the finest local ingredients.

Make sure that you try the warm Mediterranean salad, which is made with incredibly fresh local scallops, mussels, octopus, prawns, kalamata olives, tomato, potato and pepper. Ask for the outside table to dine by the infinity pool in the mangrove forest.

Chikle Prehispanic Cooking Classes

+52 998 167 0291 - chikle.com.mx
Carlos Salinas de Gortari, Alfredo V. Bonfil, Cancun, Mexico
21° 5' 4.6068" N 86° 51' 26.0244" W

This photo of Chikle Prehispanic Cooking Classes is courtesy of TripAdvisor

This is a fascinating way to learn the secrets of the cuisine of the ancient Mayans. It's not all about chili peppers, you'll learn how to make intriguing dishes involving peanuts, coconut, vanilla and other mouthwatering ingredients.

These cooking classes actually take place deep in the jungle and are hosted by indigenous chefs. The classes are small, so it's a great place to learn about the culture.

Taco Tours

+52 998 845 2091 - taco-tour.com
Av. Coba 9, Chedraui Department Store, Downtown, Cancun, Mexico
21°09'27.5"N 86°49'32.9"W

This photo of Taco Tour is courtesy of TripAdvisor

It can sometimes be difficult to know where the authentic restaurants are and where the locals eat, but this tour promises to give you the insider take on Cancun. Just sign up for your tour at taco-tour.com and you will be guided to downtown locations where you can experience the authentic taste of Mexican cuisine.

You'll have the chance to stuff your face with a lot of tacos on this tour, all brimming with fresh and delicious ingredients. There is even a vegetarian taco tour as well.

Parque las Palapas

24 hours
5 Alcatraces, Sm 22, Benito Juárez, 77500
21° 9' 40.2804" N 86° 49' 39.972" W

Image Source: Shinya Suzuki

When the sun goes down, the locals and their families flock to this chill park to chow down on food from local street stalls. There are always buskers around performing live music, setting the scene for a lively evening.

The daily special prices are extremely cheap and the food is tasty and authentic. This is your chance to eat real authentic Mexican street food and see how the locals hang out in their spare time.

Va Q' Va

+52 998 255 7435 - 10am to 7pm - vaqva.com.mx Region 220 Mz. 38 Lt. 18-19, 77517
21° 10' 9.5232" N 86° 52' 7.3488" W

This photo of Va Q' Va is courtesy of Tripadvisor

If you have a craving for authentic Mexican seafood, this little-known spot in a slightly obscure area of downtown Cancun will blow you out of the water. It is a large indoor-outdoor eatery that is packed with locals all throughout the weekend.

The fish is fresh and flavorful and you can have it cooked many different ways (or uncooked, if you are a ceviche fan). Wash it all down with a refreshing michelada and soak up the lively atmosphere.

Drink

There is a reason why Cancun has a reputation for being a spring break destination - it has plenty of places to get your drink on. However, they aren't all frat boy party spots - there are plenty of cool laid back bars, friendly pubs and sophisticated joints too. Here are some of the best places in Cancun where you can relax and unwind with something delicious and refreshing.

The Tequila Herradura Sensorial Museum

+52 998 176 8203
Blvd. Kukulcan km 12.5, zona hotelera
En El Segundo Piso de la Tienda la Europea, Cancun 77500
21° 6' 26.2224" N 86° 45' 47.0124" W

If you can't stomach tequila ever since you went a bit overboard during spring break in college, this attraction might not be for you. However, if you are keen on the classic Mexican spirit and you want to learn a little more about how it is made, check out the Tequila museum.

You can take an hour and 20 minute long tour that will reveal the history of the iconic Herradura brand. You'll see how tequila is distilled, learn about proper drinking etiquette and get to taste a range of different tequilas. Don't forget the lime and the salt!

Las de Guanatos

+52 1 998 280 8031 - 12pm to 2:30am - Facebook Page
Plaza Kabah, Av. Kabah, Mz. 1 Lt. 401 02, Local 14 FB,
Supermanzana 248
21° 11' 13.6932" N 86° 52' 3.0144" W

You can't have a trip to Mexico without drinking at least one margarita (or ten) - it would simply be wrong. Invented in Mexico in the 1930s, the well known tequila based cocktail is synonymous with kicking back in the sunshine and switching to vacation mode.

If you have only one margarita on your trip to Cancun, make it the one at Las de Guanatos. At this chill bar they serve margaritas with aged tequila and hints of orange, with tamarind or salt on the rim. If you feel hungry after a few glasses, you can also try the house-made rolled tacos.

The Surfin' Burrito

+52 998 883 0083 - 24 Hours - Facebook Page
Blvd. Kukulcan Km. 9.5, Zona Hotelera, 77500
21° 7' 56.4888" N 86° 44' 49.884" W

This photo of The Surfin Burrito is courtesy of TripAdvisor

Who doesn't like beach bars? This lively little spot is known for it's great food and it's open location right up against the sand.. It's also great if you want to enjoy some cheap tequila shots and refreshing cold beers while chatting with surfers.

There is a bus that runs on a regular basis from the main hotel area to Surfin' Burrito and the bar never closes.

El Rincon del Vino

+52 998 898 2446 - 1pm to 1am, 6pm to 1pm on Sat - Facebook Page
Náder 88, 77500 Benito Juárez, Q.R
21° 9' 39.888" N 86° 49' 26.4" W

This photo of El Rincon del Vino is courtesy of Tripadvisor

So you've had tequila, margaritas and beer - the classic things to drink while you are in Mexico. But what about wine? Wine might not be the first drink that comes to mind when you imagine Cancun, but El Rincon del Vino is establishing itself as a classy wine bar with a top notch selection of superb vintages.

It focuses mostly on Argentinian, Chilean and Mexican wines and there is often a live band to set the mood while you sip. Oh, and it's a perfect place to take someone on a date if you want to really impress them.

Horchata

Though not a place, Horchata is so quintessential, it deserves a dedicated shout-out in our Drink chapter.

Another typical Mexican drink that you must try on your visit, Horchata is an iced beverage made from ground rice. Sweet and milky, you will usually see it at an authentic Mexican restaurant in a large jar. It is usually served with a big ladle, scooped straight from the jar into your glass. While not usually made with alcohol, you can add some rum to turn it into a boozy but refreshing treat.

Horchata is to Mexicans like Lemonade is to Americans as it tastes amazing in the summer when you need to beat the heat, and is often sweetened with sugar, vanilla and cinnamon. It has a very smooth texture and is served at most traditional Mexican restaurants in Cancun. Sadly most tourists don't order it because they don't know what it is, but like margarita's, you have to experience it at least once. For the best horchata you should head outside of the hotel zone and find the restaurants where there are more locals than gringos.

Isla Brewing Company

+52 998 257 8711 - 10am to 6pm - islabrewing.com
Jesús Martínez Ross 62, Q. Roo, 77400 Isla Mujeres, Q.R.
21° 14' 9.3444" N 86° 43' 59.3004" W

Image Source - Isla Brewing Company

Would you have guessed that you would find a brewery on a tiny island? When you take the short ferry over to the laid back and charming Isla Mujeres, make sure to stop at Isla Brewing to sample some of the craft brews - such as the Sleepy Iguana Caribbean Pale Ale or the Landlubber English Pale Ale.

This brewery was founded by Jeff & Rhett McGahee, who are originally from North Carolina but fell in love with Mexico. Like many guys from Asheville, Jeff brewed at home within a vibrant community of beer enthusiasts. He brought his passion with him when the family moved to Isla Mujeres with their daughter.

Experience

If your idea of fun is to leave your comfort zone behind and try something new and exciting, Cancun is the perfect tropical adventure playground.

There are plenty of experiences here that will take you beyond the ordinary - from hovering with a jetpack to swimming with whale sharks to horseback riding. You'll get your adrenaline flowing and your blood pumping, making that beer on the beach afterwards so much more well-earned.

Here are some of the most thrilling activities you can enjoy in Cancun to help create the best memories!

Fly with Jetpack Adventures

+52 998 254 3956 - 9am to 6pm - jetpackadventures.com
La Isla Shopping Village, Blvd. Kukulcán Km 12.5, Zona Hotelera,
77500 Cancún, Q.R., Mexico
21° 6' 35.6472" N 86° 45' 51.6924" W

Image source: jetpackadventures.com

Have you ever wondered what it would be like to be able to fly like the Rocketeer or George Jetson? At Jetpack Adventures you will be strapped into a pack with a powerful jet of water shooting out of it, which will allow you to hover above the surface of the ocean.

This is one of the newer experiences in Cancun and the TripAdvisor page is filled with thrilled customers raving about the sensation of hovering in the air. Do you have the courage to give it a try? DO YA?!

BT Dubz srsly fun vid here: https://www.youtube.com/watch?v=NliKe_zh9kg

Dive the Cancun Underwater Museum

21.1351° N, 86.7537° W

By 2il org [CC BY 2.0], via Flickr

Immerse yourself in the quirky culture of Cancun as you dive beneath the water to explore this strange and beautiful attraction. It is the work of one devoted environmentalist and sculptor - Jason deCaires Taylor. He has created 450 statues that are on display deep beneath the waves between Cancun and Isla Mujeres.

The sculptures aren't just beautiful - they also serve a purpose. They create an artificial reef that gives coral a place to grow. Also, they distract scuba divers and divert them away from some very sensitive areas of natural coral located nearby.

Some companies that offer tours and equipment:

Coconut Divers
Address: Blvd. Kukulcan Km 5.8, Zona Hotelera, 77500
Cancún, Q.R., Mexico
Hours: 8:30AM-5PM
Phone: +52 998 883 1484

Aquaworld Cancun
Address: Boulevard Kukulcan km 15.3, Zona Hotelera, 77500
Cancún, Mexico
Hours: 7AM-8PM
Phone: +52 998 848 8326

Scuba Diving Cancun
Address: KM 3.5, Boulevard Kukulcan, Zona Hotelera, 77520
Cancún, Q.R., Mexico
Hours: 8:30AM-5AM
Phone: +52 1 998 228 5335

And here's the Googs for more!

Swim in a Cenote

Image source: savvysugar.com pinterest

Cenotes are hidden underground sinkholes filled with cool clear water. These underground caves and rivers were incredibly important sources of water for ancient civilisations. Many of them were only discovered recently due to limestone cave-in's, creating holes within the earth, leading to pockets of clear turquoise water.

You can snorkel through the caverns and rock formations to discover strange underwater life, lush vegetation, turtles and fish. Ik Kil is one of the most convenient cenotes to reach from Cancun as it is en route to the Mayan ruins at Chichen Itza. Another must-see cenote is Dos Ojos, which is a system of caverns extending deep into the earth and a very popular destination for SCUBA divers.

Check this awesome video from Sir Ryan Van Duzer, which has some great shots of some Cenotes, also featuring Ryan's fun, energetic and goofball filming style, which we've come to love.

And for even more awesome Cenotes, Thrillist put together this rad list!

Cenote Pet Cemetery Snorkel Adventure

+52 984 169 3763 - cenotessacactun.com
Cenotes Sac Actun, Tulum
20°19'03.8"N 87°24'35.0"W

This photo of Yucatan Diving & Travel is courtesy of TripAdvisor

This might be one of the strangest experiences you can have in Cancun. The bones of dead animals, tossed into a cave and hidden for centuries, were recently discovered by a team of divers.

Within an underground cenote in the Dos Ojos cave system there is a cave with a soft sandy surface, which hid these animal bones, ranging from ancient creatures to modern animals. Scientists found some pretty incredible things down there, from the lower jawbone of a tapir to the remains of a prehistoric camel… WTH?!

The site, now known as the Pet Cemetery, was thought by scientists to have been used as a disposal pit long before the water table rose. It is possible to SCUBA dive and snorkel at the site, although it is a challenging dive with fragile rock formations on all sides. If you are not a confident scuba diver you might want to stick to snorkeling and preserve the site for future visitors.

Cuddle a Crocodile!

+52 998 850 3719 - 9am to 5pm - crococunzoo.com
Carretera Cancun - Tulum Km 31, 77580
21° 9' 12.5748" N 86° 49' 30.5544" W

Have you ever wanted to get up close and cuddle a crocodile? No?!

Crococun Zoo is a very cool local wildlife center that protects endangered species including butterflies, spiders, coatis, monkeys, parrots, deer and of course, crocodiles.

You will be taken on a guided tour with your English speaking guide and have the chance to hold, touch and feed the wild local animals.

The official website states that you will "Feel emotions you have never felt, with creatures you have never met." Sounds pretty great, doesn't it? Time to toughen up and make some new croc and spidey friends! Or maybe just play with the monkeys. Up to you.

Selvatica: ATV and Zipline Adventures

+52 998 881 3030 - 9am to 5pm - selvatica.com.mx
Ruta de los cenotes Km 18, Carretera Puerto Morelos - Leona Vicario, 77580 Puerto Morelos, Q.R
20° 55' 28.4376" N 87° 7' 41.5632" W

This photo of Selvatica is courtesy of TripAdvisor

Feel the wind rushing in your face as you zoom along a zipline, high above the lush green forest canopy. At this theme Adventure Park, you will be able to soar through the treetops at high speed, while safely strapped into your harness. Then, you will be taken on a tour through the remote wild jungle on an ATV. After all of that excitement, you will go for a swim in a beautiful forest pool to relax and unwind. How could it get more perfect than that?

Horseback Riding at Rancho Baaxal

+52 1 984 145 8962 - 9am to 6pm - ranchobaaxal.com
Solidaridad, Punta Maroma, Quintana Roo, Mexico
20° 44' 16.0008" N 86° 58' 3" W

This photo of Rancho Baaxal is courtesy of Tripadvisor

Imagine riding through the lush and humid Mexican jungle, the rich tropical foliage all around you and the chattering of the birds filling the air. Rancho Baaxal is a superb spot for a horseback riding adventure and the owners of the ranch have a deep love for nature which reflects in everything they do.

Your horseback journey will take you all the way to Maroma Beach, which has been named by Travel Channel as one of the Top Ten Most Beautiful Beaches in the World - for four years in a row. If you are feeling adventurous you could even take a Full Moon Tour - an unforgettable adventure out underneath the stars.

Swimming with Whale Sharks

Image courtesy of EcoColors Whake Shark Tour Cancun

Whale sharks are the largest fish in the world - they can reach up to 45 feet in length! Don't worry though, they are more interested in eating plankton for dinner than you, so have no fear when you swim with them!

Being relaxed and gentle beasts, they'll let you get up close and swim around them, which is quite a remarkable experience. If you are visiting Cancun during whale shark season (May to September) you won't want to miss out on this experience, trust.

Miss Kassandra Brooks kindly created a very well made video of the experience, complete with some whale shark info and tips here!

Numerous tour companies in Cancun can arrange a full day tour, complete with wetsuits and lunch on the boat. Here's one which focuses specifically on the wonderful Whale Shark beasties:

Cancun Whale Shark Tours
Website: cancunwhalesharktours.com
Address: Carretera a Punta Sam Km. 1,5, Puerto Juárez, 77500 Cancún, Q.R., Mexico
Hours: 8AM-8PM
Phone: (305) 433-7523

Relax & Chill

Sometimes the exciting, non-stop pace of life in Cancun can get a little overwhelming and you need to take a day just to recharge dem batts. Fortunately, there are pockets of peaceful tranquility within Cancun where you can hide until #adventuremode strikes again. Here are a few of the most relaxing spots!

Parque Kabah

+52 998 206 1356 - 6am to 6pm - parquekabah.blogspot.mx
Av Nichupte, Benito Juárez, 77500 Cancún, Q.R., Mexico
21° 8' 27.0204" N 86° 51' 21.654" W

This Photo of Parque Kabah is courtesy of UnionCancun.mx

When you want to escape from the noise and traffic of the city, head to Parque Kabah, a green oasis of solitude only around 15 minutes walk from the city centre. Locals often come here to walk, run or just sit and enjoy nature. The park is alive with wildlife and spider monkeys swinging through the trees!

Filled with palm trees and lush vegetation you could sit by the pond and watch the turtles swim for hours. You might also spot several colourful parrots chillin' in the trees as well. So choice, even Bueller would approve.

Leblanc Spa Resort

800-986-5632 - leblancsparesort.com
Boulevard Kukulcan Km.10, Zona Hotelera, 77500 Cancun, JAL, Mexico
21° 8' 5.1036" N 86° 45' 32.8392" W

This photo of Le Blanc Spa Resort is courtesy of TripAdvisor

If you are feeling a little bit frazzled from the stress of the trail and adventure and want to give your body and mind a complete reset - this spa will make you feel brand new again. It's one of the most well known spas in Cancun thanks to it's gorgeous nature-inspired design and top notch service.

As you stroll along the polished stone walkways through the columns of white chiffon, you'll start to feel yourself relaxing. After you have been treated to the warm and cold pools, steam room, sauna and hydro-reflexology pool you'll get the sensation that you are floating on a cloud.

Xbalamque

+52 998 193 2720 - 24 hours - xbalamque.com
Av. Yaxchilan No. 31 Mza. 18 Lt. 18 SM. 22, Zona Centro, 77500
Cancún, QROO, Mexico
21° 9' 42.2604" N 86° 49' 44.8716" W

This photo of Hotel Xbalamque Resort & Spa is courtesy of TripAdvisor

How did the ancient's relax when they were stressed out? You can unwind the Mayan way at this small yet welcoming spa in the legendary Xbalamque Hotel. It features ancient cleansing rituals and spa treatments from regional cultures, at surprisingly affordable prices.

For example, you could try the Temazcal Therapy - an immersive Mayan sweat lodge experience that uses medicinal herbs and meditative instruction to cleanse your mind and renew your mental energy.

Yoga Classes on the Beach

877-845-3795 - villapalmarcancun.com
Carretera a Punta Sam Km 5.2 Manzana 9 Lote 3 SM 2, Zona Continental de Isla Mujeres
21° 13' 54.9012" N 86° 48' 13.9968" W

This photo of Villa del Palmar Cancun Beach Resort & Spa is courtesy of TripAdvisor

Imagine stretching into downward dog while listening to the waves lapping at the shore. What could be more relaxing than taking a yoga class on the beach?

With Villa del Palmar Cancun offering yoga classes every other day, you can practice your sun salutations while watching the sun rise over the ocean, an incredible experience.

Mats and towels are provided, so all you have to do is show up at the beachfront terrace with a bottle of water and an open mind.

Garrafon Natural Reef Park

+52 998 193 3370 - 9am to 6pm - garrafon.com
Camino Sac Bajo, Lote 26, Paraíso Laguna Mar, 77400 Isla Mujeres
21° 14' 5.2332" N 86° 44' 28.626" W

Photo Source: Kirt Edblom via Flickr

Unwind from the crazy noise of the city by going for a calming and relaxing walk along any of the series of trails above the reefs in Garrafon Natural Reef Park.

The way this beautiful walkway has been designed makes it feel like you are standing in the middle of the great blue wild ocean. It is beautiful, humbling and will make you feel whole again, even after the craziest weekend.

You can also take the opportunity while you're here to get face to face with a dolphin!

Isla Mujeres

21° 13' 55.848" N 86° 44' 2.7348" W

By Christine Zenino CC Wikimedia 2.0

It's name means "Island of Women" and it is only a 20 minute ferry ride from Cancun.

Offering a completely different atmosphere from the hustle and bustle of the city, it's the perfect place to relax in between adventures. It gets its name from the statues of women that Spanish conqueror Francisco Hernandez de Cordoba saw on the Mayan temples on the island.

Visiting Isla Mujeres is a must while you're in Cancun as it offers a much more laid back atmosphere and a chance to relax to balance out all the wild nights and adventurous day trips. You can visit the turtle protection center, swim with dolphins and dine at one of the absolutely gorgeous beachside restaurants.

Hostels & Hospitality Exchanges

We've listed some fancy digs and some fair priced hotels already, however for those who prefer to spend their dough on experiences rather than sleeping quarters, here's some resources.

Hostels

Here's some useful sites for finding and booking hostels:

- hostelbookers.com
- hostelworld.com
- hostels.com

Here's a handful of hostels we loved in Cancun which are affordable and fun:

Hostel Natura Cancún - Dorms about $22, Rooms $28+
+52 998 883 0585
Blvd. Kukulcan Km 9.5, Zona Hotelera, 77500 Cancún, Q.R., Mexico
21°07'47.7"N 86°44'59.1"W

Granada 6 - Dorms around $12, Rooms around $28
+52 998 310 1856
Granada No. 6 MZ 8, SM 2A, 77500 Cancún, QROO, Mexico
21°10'02.7"N 86°49'21.1"W

Las Flores - Dorms around $9, Rooms $22+
+52 998 130 2671
Calle Palmera no. 63 MZ 8 Lt 1, 77500 Cancún, Q.R., Mexico
21°09'54.9"N 86°49'44.0"W

Hospitality Exchanges

Here's a handful of websites we've found helpful, they help you to check if there's anywhere you can stay for free!

- couchsurfing.com
- globalfreeloaders.com
- hospitalityclub.org
- stay4free.com

Traveling Knowledge

Checklists

Preflight

1. Is your Passport valid or expired?
2. Do you need a Visa to enter Cancun? (most don't, but just in case…)
3. Inform your Credit card, debit card and bank(s) of your travel plans so you don't get a hold put on for fraud!
4. Up to date on your vaccines?
5. Travel Insurance?
6. Cell phone international plan purchased?

Make sure to pack...

1. Passport!!
2. Credit and debit cards, US currency (use our budgeting section to plan how much)
3. Device chargers, cell phone
4. Kindle or a good ol' fashioned paper book for the flight
5. Drivers License, if you intend to rent a car
6. Sunblock
7. Insect repellant
8. Swimsuit(s)
9. Translator app/Phrasebook
10. Camera
11. Multitool or knife (not in your carry on!)
12. Flashlight or Headlamp
13. Snorkeling stuff
14. Toiletries

Language

Spanish mostly, and some speaking the old language, Maya

Currency, Banks & Exchange Rates

Mexican Peso. Banks and ATM's are pretty much everywhere in the larger and medium neighborhoods and most places in them accept cards as well.

We definitely do suggest you carry some cash with you though as some of the best little spots are cash only. Not to mention it's a lot easier and faster to pay at a crowded bar, or really anywhere for that matter, when you can slap down some bills and split rather than having to wait your turn for your card to be ran.

For the most recent exchange rates or your country is not listed below, check out xe.com

Here's a quick table for reference (June 2017 - currency stays fairly stable, barring any major international economic upsets):

Your Currency	Mexican Peso
US Dollar	$18.22
Euro	$20.55
Canadian Dollar	$13.54
100 Japanese Yen	$16.77
Great Britain Pound	$23.53
Australian Dollar	$13.69

New Zealand Dollar	$13.10

Visas

An FMM, Forma Migratoria Multiple, is required; this is a Cancun tourist permit. You can obtain one from your travel agent, on the plane there (ask a steward if they don't give one to you before landing) or at any point of entry.

The immigration dude at the CanCun passport control area might ask you to provide proof that you have money to fly back home or have a return ticket already. Unlikely, but FYI.

The immigration peeps will also check your paperwork, stamp and process the aforementioned FMM, then give you a stub, a portion of the form. They REQUIRE that you give this stub back to them when leaving, so DON'T LOSE IT or you'll go to jail! Jk. But they will probably fine you some Pesos. Probably certainly more than you want to be fined. So keep it safe and dry. We suggest keeping it inside your passport.

Most people of our wonderful planetoid don't need a visa to enter Mexico, however a few countries are required, so it's worth making sure you're good. Below are the countries that can enter Mexico without a visa, and any others must present a visa, so it's worth checking to see if you're homeland is listed.

Andorra, Argentina, Australia, Austria, Belgium, Canada, Chile, Costa Rica, Cyprus, Czech Republic, Denmark, Estonia, Finland, France, Germany,Greece, Hong Kong,Hungary, Ireland, Island, Israel, Italy, Japan, Latvia, Liechtenstein, Lithuania, Luxembourg, Malta, Monaco, Netherlands, New Zealand, Norway, Poland,

Portugal, San Marino, Singapore, Slovakia, Slovenia, South Korea, Spain, Sweden, Switzerland, United Kingdom, Uruguay, USA,Venezuela

Phones

Most US cell companies offer very good Mexico plans, and T-Mobile has even gone as far as to offer 4G standard, without the need to purchase any international minutes or data. It's a good idea though to double check your provider's website beforehand.

Time

Yucatan, Campeche and Chiapas are the same as US Central time and -6 hours GMT/UTC. Quintana Roo is Eastern time, -5 hours.

Electricity

Standard US two or three prong outlets are the standard, at 127v/60hz

Seasons & the Best Times to Go

December to April, the popular time

It's most typical for travelers to visit Cancun and the surrounding regions during the months of December through April, as most go to get away from colder weather in the US. Same for travelers from most Western countries.

There's also more activities during these months, but also higher prices, and most hotels are known to increase their prices, some as much as double.

The climate is fairly steady, however it does get hotter in the summer… but isn't that the point? =)

Doesn't rain much either and the only really big thing to take note of is the 'Nortes', aka Northerly Winds, which can make it a bit chilly sometimes if you're not prepared or your camping. Also keep them in mind when you're hiking on precarious areas. They don't care how assured or weak your footing is.

July & August, their mid season

This is in between the high season and slow season, where hotel prices are rising and tourists/frequent visitors are rising. Some deals can be found but not many. Mexicans that have a higher heat tolerance than gringo's and english gents jump over to the beaches for vacay.

It's very hot and humid, so keep that in mind, so if you don't like Florida, don't visit during these months. If you love the humidity and frizzy hair, go for it.

Slow Seasons, May & June and September to November

For the savvy and budget minded traveler, as funny as it may sound, going just before summer and during the fall is smart, as you can get some pretty incredible deals.

If you're the type to prefer taking advantage of more authentic offerings than the popular tourist attractions, these are the best months for you. Less crowded attractions, ruins and hotels make for a much more enjoyable visit.

Arriving

There's four airports you can arrive through, which you should decide between based on your activities. There's one website for all of them: http://www.asur.com.mx and here's a bit of essential info for each:

Aeropuerto International de Cancun

+52 55 5284 0400
Carretera Cancún-Chetumal Km 22, 77565 Cancún, Q.R., Mexico
21.036442, -86.877823

Taxi's charge about 500 pesos, or about 28 US, to take you to the Ciudad Cancun or Zona Hotelera areas, however shuttles leave often, such as the Super Shuttle and the Green Line, charge about 160 pesos, or about $9 us, to get to. ADO buses also zip straight to the downtown bus station and cost only about 64 pesos or about $3.50 US.

Aeropuerto International de Merida

+52 999 940 6090
Carretera Mérida a Uman Km 4,5, 97291 Mérida, Yuc., Mexico
20.933961, -89.663606

Taxi's out front of the airport usually charge around 200 pesos, or about $11 US, to get to downtown Cancun. Buses charge around 7 pesos, or about half a buck, but don't enter the airport; you'll have to walk out and wait for one on the main road.

Cozumel International Airport

+52 987 872 2081
Boulevard Aeropuerto Cozumel s/n, 77600 San Miguel de Cozumel, Q.R., Mexico
20.511229, -86.930485

57 pesos or about 3 US for a shuttle from the airport into town. If you'd rather just stay on the island, their hotels are about 97 to 140 pesos, or 5 to 8 bucks a night.

Tuxtla Gutiérrez International Airport

+52 961 615 5060
Francisco Sarabia, 29176 Chiapa de Corzo, Chis., Mexico
16.563637, -93.013406

Small buses run from this airport to San Cristobal de las Casas' bus terminal, and from there you can get anywhere you need to go.

Important Phone Codes & Numbers

Codes

1 before long distance and toll free numbers
44 & the city code before cell phones
45 for long distance cell phone calls

Numbers

Country Code	52
Directory Assistance	040
Emergencies	066
International Access	00 and 011 from USA and

Code	CAN
Roadside Assistance	078
Domestic Operator	020
International Operator	090

Budgeting

If you're the type to think and plan ahead, no doubt you're also the type to want to set a budget for your trip. To figure out amounts to set aside here's a quick table that should help (dorms/hotels are per night, car rental per day):

Penny the Pincher

Thing	Pesos	Dollars
Dorm room bed	150-220	8 - 12
Double room in simple motel	400-500	20 - 28
Street grub & taqueria's	20-60	1 - 4
City bus	4-10	.20 - .60

Bobby the Baller on a Budget

Thing	Pesos	Dollars
Double room in comfy	600 -	30 - 65

hotel	1200	
Lunch or Dinner sit down	80 - 160	5 - 10
Taxi trip in the city	20 - 60	1 - 4
Adventures, sightseeing	100 - 250	5 - 15

Mikey's Makin It Rain

Thing	Pesos	Dollars
Double room in fancy hotel	1200 & up	65 & up
Fine dining	250 - 500	15 - 30
Car rental w basic insurance	500 & up	30 & up
Guided tours	1000 - 2500	55 - 140

Operating Hours & Months

During the high season most places are open long hours to collect as much mula as possible, however in the mid season, most shops, tours, restaurants etc. decrease their hours, and in the off season, many close entirely for weeks or months at a time. Don't stress though if you are planning on going in the off season, however, as there is still plenty to do and see, and the main stuff every visitor should mark off the budget list is usually available/open.

The typical hours for places during the high season are 9am to 5pm. Here's a bit more detail:

Ruins	8am to 5pm

sites	
Banks	9am to 5pm, some open half day on Saturday
Cafe's	8am to 9pm
Cenotes	9am to 5pm
Museums	9am to 5pm Tuesday to Sunday

Tipping

It's pretty different in Cancun! Here's a handy table to know what to tip to whom:

Person/Place	**Pesos/Percentage**
Restaurants	If not included in check, 15%
Taxi's	Don't have to tip them, but if if you take advantage of an extra service, like carrying bags, you should tip them some Pesos
Bartenders	Unlike most countries, the bartenders usually don't get tipped, so you don't need to. But they sure appreciate it if you do!
Hotel staff	5-10% of room costs
Supermarket baggers & gas station attendants	3 - 5
Porters (per bag)	25

Getting Around

It's very easy to get around Cancun and the whole region. Shuttles are everywhere, taxi's are pretty cheap and buses even cheaper. If you want to spend the $, you can rent a car for about $750 pesos, or about 40-50 US, a day.

Bike Around Cancun - City or Mountain Bicycle Rental
+52 998 8302934
Website: fabikearoundcancun.wixsite.com/bikearoundcancun
21°07'57.5"N 86°44'46.3"W

Printed in Great Britain
by Amazon

27139481R00064